CLASSIC RIDES

CLASSIC Chargers

BY CLAIRE ROMAINE

I0891781

INVESTIGATE!

Enslow PUBLISHING

Please visit our website, www.enslow.com. For a free color catalog of all our high-quality books, call toll free 1-800-398-2504 or fax 1-877-980-4454.

Cataloging-in-Publication Data

Names: Romaine, Claire.
Title: Classic Chargers / Claire Romaine.
Description: New York : Enslow Publishing, 2021. | Series: Classic rides | Includes glossary and index.
Identifiers: ISBN 9781978517912 (pbk.) | ISBN 9781978517936 (library bound) | ISBN 9781978517929 (6 pack)
Subjects: LCSH: Dodge Charger automobile–Juvenile literature. | Muscle cars–United States–History–Juvenile literature.
Classification: LCC TL215.D6 R66 2021 | DDC 629.222'2–dc23

Published in 2021 by
Enslow Publishing
101 West 23rd Street, Suite #240
New York, NY 10011

Copyright © 2021 Enslow Publishing

Designer: Katelyn E. Reynolds
Editor: Therese Shea

Photo credits: Cover, p. 1 (left Charger) yauhenka/Shutterstock.com; cover, p. 1 (middle Charger) Grzegorz Czapski/Shutterstock.com; cover, p. 1 (right Charger) Ken Morris/Shutterstock.com; cover, pp. 1–32 (series chrome font) Mott Jordan/Shutterstock.com; cover, pp. 1–32 (series background) Sylvie Bouchard/Shutterstock.com; p. 5 (main) Darryl Norenberg/The Enthusiast Network via Getty Images/Getty Images; p. 5 (inset) Bettmann/Getty Images; pp. 7 (main), 14, 17, 23 (inset) Steve Lagreca/Shutterstock.com; p. 7 (inset) Jonathan Gibbs (FastbackJon)/Arkz86/Wikipedia.org; p. 8 Heritage Images/Hulton Archive/Getty Images; p. 9 Tony Savino/Shutterstock.com; p. 10 Chase Clausen/Shutterstock.com; p. 11 Baranov E/Shutterstock.com; p. 13 ISC Images & Archives via Getty Images; p. 15 ISC Archives/CQ-Roll Call Group via Getty Images; p. 19 (main) David J. Becker/Getty Images; p. 19 (inset) yauhenka/Shutterstock.com; p. 20 Ollie Millington/Getty Images; p. 21 Greg Gjerdingen (https://www.flickr.com/people/52900873@N07) from Willmar, USA/OceanAtoll/Wikipedia.org; p. 23 (main) Darren Brode/Shutterstock.com; p. 25 Ed Aldridge/Shutterstock.com; p. 27 Barry Blackburn/Shutterstock.com; p. 29 Lissandra Melo/Shutterstock.com.

Portions of this work were originally authored by Michael Portman and published as *Chargers*. All new material this edition authored by Claire Romaine.

All rights reserved. No part of this book may be reproduced in any form without permission in writing from the publisher, except by a reviewer.

Printed in the United States of America

Some of the images in this book illustrate individuals who are models. The depictions do not imply actual situations or events.

CPSIA compliance information: Batch #BS20ENS: For further information contact Enslow Publishing, New York, New York, at 1-800-398-2504.

Find us on

Contents

WORDS IN THE GLOSSARY APPEAR IN **BOLD** TYPE THE FIRST TIME THEY ARE USED IN THE TEXT.

THE MUSCLE CAR

Market

In the 1960s, carmakers battled to produce a car that would top the muscle car market. Muscle car was the name for an affordable, midsize vehicle with a powerful engine. People had been making their own muscle cars by placing big engines in regular cars they bought and even racing them.

GET THE FACTS!

Brothers Horace and John Dodge founded the Dodge car brand in 1913. They sold 250 vehicles in 1914 and 45,000 the next year. In 1928, Dodge was sold to the Chrysler Corporation, which is now owned by the Fiat SpA company.

Carmakers, including Dodge, saw an opportunity for a new kind of factory-produced car. Dodge used the same platform it was using for its Dodge Coronet as well as powerful engines to produce its now **classic** muscle car, the Charger.

1966 DODGE CORONET

THE CHARGER (BELOW) LOOKED SPORTIER THAN THE CORONET, EVEN THOUGH THEY SHARED A PLATFORM. A PLATFORM IS THE NAME FOR A CAR'S OVERALL **DESIGN** AND COLLECTION OF PARTS.

THE FIRST Chargers

The first generation, or class, of Dodge Chargers began in 1966. They were fastbacks, which means they sported a roof that sloped down in the back. Chargers were built using the Chrysler B-body platform, and they were bigger than most muscle cars. Dodge offered several engine choices to power a car this large, including its famous racing engine, the 426 Hemi.

GET THE FACTS!

The inside of the 1966 and 1967 Dodge Chargers was modern for the time. It featured four separate seats called bucket seats, and the rear seats folded down for extra room. The instrument panel held four dials that glowed in the dark!

THE FIRST GENERATION OF DODGE CHARGERS HAD HEADLIGHTS HIDDEN BEHIND THE GRILLE. THE GRILLE IS THE METAL SCREEN ON THE FRONT OF A CAR THAT ALLOWS COOL AIR INTO THE ENGINE.

The 1966 model sold well, so few changes were made in the 1967 model year. When the 1967 model sold poorly, Dodge knew it was time to rework the car.

SECOND-GENERATION

Chargers

Though the second generation of Chargers kept the B-body, it had a new look. The car was longer and seemed to lean forward. The **fenders** curved around the tires. The Charger looked fast, even when it was standing still!

THE DODGE CHARGER R/T WAS FEATURED IN A FAMOUS CAR CHASE SCENE IN THE 1968 MOVIE *BULLITT*.

But muscle cars aren't only about looks. In 1968, Dodge introduced the high-performance Charger R/T, which stands for Road/Track. The Charger R/T featured heavy-duty brakes and **suspension**, as well as wider tires. Engine choices, including the 440 Magnum and the 426 Hemi, offered plenty of **horsepower**.

GET THE FACTS!

The Charger offered features many cars have today, such as ***cruise control****. However, it wasn't* ***fuel-efficient****. For example, a 1968 Dodge Charger R/T with a 426 Hemi got only about 8 miles per gallon (3.4 km per liter).*

Many consider second-generation Chargers to be the best-looking Chargers, and the 1969 Charger is thought to be the best of these. It looked similar to the 1968 model, but it had a center divider in the grille and redesigned taillights. It was also the first Dodge to offer a power sunroof.

GET THE FACTS!

The shape of the second-generation Charger looks similar to a glass cola bottle. This shape was popular in muscle cars during the 1960s and 1970s. In fact, a 1969 Pontiac GTO could be mistaken for a 1969 Dodge Charger!

The 1970 model was the last of the second generation. Dodge did little to change it. However, the Charger's length was bumped up 1 inch (2.5 cm). The center grille divider was removed, and a bumper surrounded the grille.

THE 1968 AND 1969 CHARGERS SOLD WELL, BUT THE 1970 MODEL (BELOW) WASN'T AS SUCCESSFUL.

A NASCAR Competitor

In order for Dodge to compete in NASCAR (National Association for Stock Car Auto Racing) with its Charger, some major changes had to be made to its design. The 1969 Charger's shape caused it to be unstable and unsafe at high speeds. A newly designed grille and rear window fixed these problems, and the Charger 500 was born.

GET THE FACTS!

NASCAR rules stated that changes to a race car could be made only if at least 500 production models received the same changes. The 1966 Charger was the first U.S. production car to offer a spoiler, the plate that helps keep it stable while racing.

However, though the Charger 500 won a few races in 1969, it wasn't as successful as Dodge had hoped. It's thought that only 392 Dodge 500s were sold to the public.

A SPOILER MAY BE PLACED IN THE FRONT OR REAR OF THE CAR. THE DODGE CHARGER 500'S WAS UNDER THE FRONT BUMPER.

A WINGED Wonder

Dodge's next shot at a winning race car was the Charger Daytona. The problem with the Charger 500's performance continued to be its shape, not its engine. So, Dodge added a long, wedge-shaped grille that made it more **aerodynamic**. The Charger Daytona's only purpose was to win races, and that's exactly what it did!

GET THE FACTS!

The most noticeable thing about the Charger Daytona was the 23-inch (58 cm) rear spoiler. Dodge used special wind tunnels to test the aerodynamics of its cars with air currents. After much testing, the giant winged spoiler was found to be the best design.

The Dodge Charger Daytona won its very first race in 1969, the Talladega 500. In 1970, the Charger Daytona became the first car in NASCAR history to complete a lap at more than 200 miles (322 km) per hour!

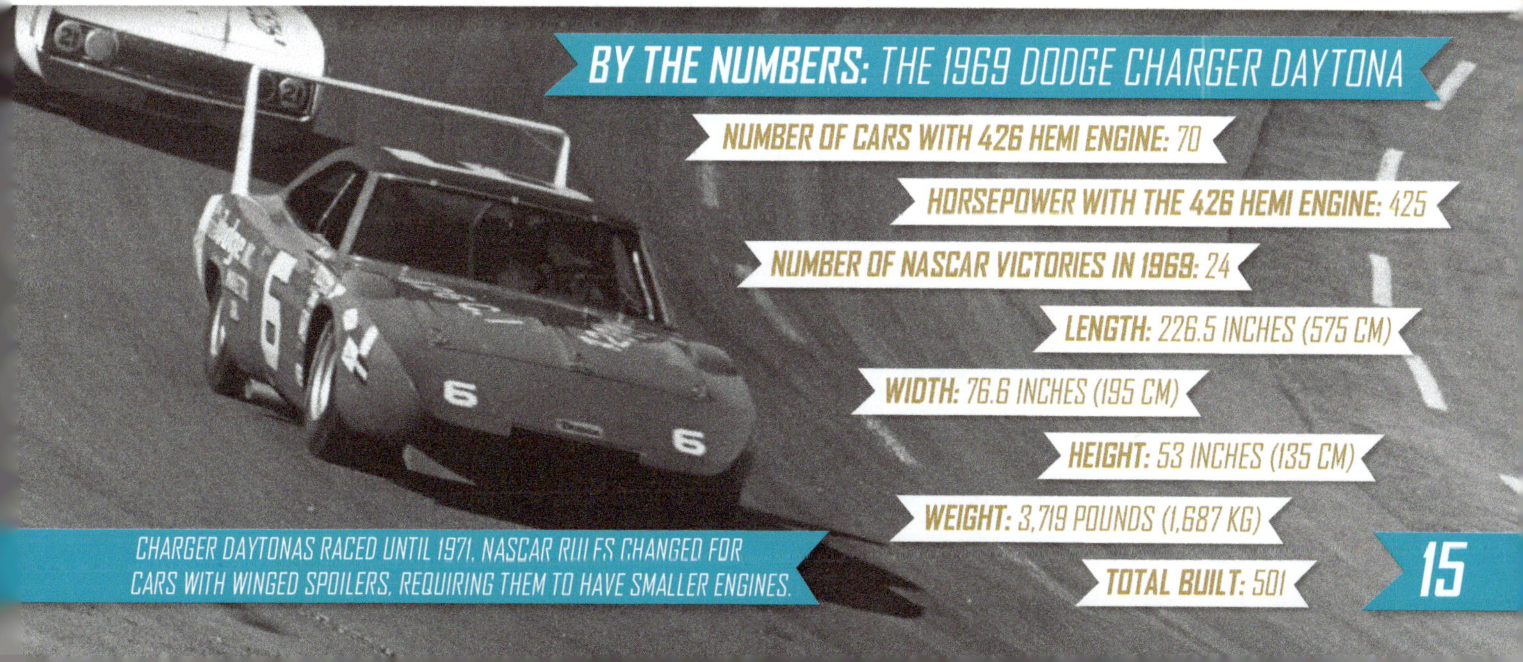

BY THE NUMBERS: THE 1969 DODGE CHARGER DAYTONA

- **NUMBER OF CARS WITH 426 HEMI ENGINE:** 70
- **HORSEPOWER WITH THE 426 HEMI ENGINE:** 425
- **NUMBER OF NASCAR VICTORIES IN 1969:** 24
- **LENGTH:** 226.5 INCHES (575 CM)
- **WIDTH:** 76.6 INCHES (195 CM)
- **HEIGHT:** 53 INCHES (135 CM)
- **WEIGHT:** 3,719 POUNDS (1,687 KG)
- **TOTAL BUILT:** 501

CHARGER DAYTONAS RACED UNTIL 1971. NASCAR RULES CHANGED FOR CARS WITH WINGED SPOILERS, REQUIRING THEM TO HAVE SMALLER ENGINES.

CHARGER on TV

The most well-known Dodge Charger is probably the General Lee, a 1969 Charger made famous by the TV series *The Dukes of Hazzard*. From 1979 to 1985, viewers tuned in each week to watch the General Lee jump over trains, rivers, and even houses—and drive away!

GET THE FACTS!

Many of The Dukes of Hazzard cars were actually 1968 Chargers that were changed to look like 1969 Chargers! The production crew added and removed features. Interiors that were a different color were dyed to match the inside of the General Lee.

TODAY, FEWER THAN 20 OF THE ORIGINAL GENERAL LEES ARE STILL IN EXISTENCE. THEY'RE THE STARS OF SOME CLASSIC CAR SHOWS!

Of course, a Dodge Charger can't really do all those things. Trained drivers destroyed one or two Chargers every show. The exact number of Chargers used on *The Dukes of Hazzard* isn't known, but some sources believe it was over 300!

LOSING Muscle

In 1971, the Charger began its third generation. The sleeker car offered more legroom for a comfortable ride. The 1973 Charger became the best-selling Charger yet. But by 1974, engines were fast losing power as they met new laws about air pollution. Cars got longer to meet safety standards too. The muscle-car age was coming to an end.

GET THE FACTS!

While Dodge Chargers on the road were losing power, the ones on the track weren't. NASCAR Hall of Famer Richard Petty continued to drive third-generation Chargers to many victories in the 1970s, even after the fourth generation was introduced.

RICHARD PETTY'S 1974 DODGE CHARGER WAS SOLD FOR $490,000 IN 2018. HE DROVE THIS VEHICLE TO WIN 31 RACES, THE MOST VICTORIES DRIVEN IN ONE CAR IN NASCAR HISTORY.

THIRD GENERATION

The fourth-generation Dodge Chargers lasted from 1975 until 1978. They were big, boxy, and slow. The Charger had lost its muscle, and sales were poor. Instead of redesigning the Charger, Dodge decided to replace it.

THE COMEBACK Car

1970 CHARGER R/T FROM *THE FAST AND THE FURIOUS*

In 1982, the Dodge Charger returned for a fifth generation with a new body. It was a small **hatchback** with **front-wheel drive**, rather than rear-wheel drive. In other words, it wasn't a midsize muscle car! In 1987, Dodge stopped Charger production again.

GET THE FACTS!

People still remember the beginning generations of Chargers with admiration. A 1970 Charger R/T was one of the starring cars in the *Fast & Furious* movies. Older Chargers are also featured in video games such as the *Forza Motorsport* series.

The Charger returned in 2006 on a new platform, Chrysler's LX. Because of this, some consider it a first generation, instead of the sixth. Many fans of the classic Chargers were unhappy that this car was a four-door **sedan**. However, it was back to rear-wheel drive and sold well.

A REVIEWER OF THE 2006 DODGE CHARGER R/T SAID IT LOOKED "MEAN AS A BULL" ON THE ROAD!

CHARGING INTO THE *Future*

In 2011, the next generation of Chargers was truly for the classic Charger fan. It had high-horsepower muscle and a body inspired by second-generation Chargers. It also had the latest touch-screen **technology**, fuel efficiency, and a comfortable interior. Additions to the exterior included side "scoops" along the doors and taillights that crossed nearly the whole back trunk.

GET THE FACTS!

When people buy cars, including Chargers, they sometimes can choose an option package. This is a group of special features that can be added to a car that the driver might enjoy, such as special wheel covers, grilles, ***emblems****, and high-horsepower engines.*

DODGE CHARGER SRT8 MODELS CALLED SUPER BEES OFFERED HIGH PERFORMANCE—AND INTERESTING COLORS TOO! SUPER BEES WERE FIRST PRODUCED BY DODGE IN THE 1960S AND 1970S.

Models included the Dodge Charger SE, Dodge Charger R/T, and Dodge Charger R/T AWD. In 2012, the high-performance SRT8 joined the fleet, and a Charger 100th Anniversary Edition model came out in 2014 to celebrate 100 years of Dodge.

THE SRT

The top performer of the Charger's seventh generation at first was the SRT8, which boasted 470 horsepower from a 6.4-liter Hemi V-8 engine. In 2014, the "8" was dropped from the SRT8's name, and it became the Charger SRT.

In 2019, Dodge revealed its 2020 Charger SRT Hellcat Widebody. It produces 707 horsepower, reaching 60 miles (97 km) per hour in 3.6 seconds and hitting the ¼-mile (400 m) mark in 11 seconds. Dodge claims it's the fastest factory-produced sedan in the world! The vehicle's "widebody" allows wider tires for better road grip.

GET THE FACTS!

In 1966, the cost of a Dodge Charger started at about $3,100. Today, the price of a Charger R/T begins at about $38,000, while the high-performance Charger SRT Hellcat Widebody starts at about $71,000. An option package adds to these costs.

THE CHARGER SRT HELLCAT HAS AN AIR INDUCTION HOOD TO DIRECT COLD AIR INTO THE ENGINE TO INCREASE ITS POWER AND PERFORMANCE.

DODGE CHARGER GENERATIONS

GENERATION	YEARS	PLATFORM
FIRST GENERATION	1966–1967	B-BODY
SECOND GENERATION	1968–1970	B-BODY
THIRD GENERATION	1971–1974	B-BODY
FOURTH GENERATION	1975–1978	B-BODY
FIFTH GENERATION	1982–1987	L-BODY
SIXTH GENERATION	2006–2010	LX
SEVENTH GENERATION	2011–?	LD

CHARGERS on the Force

Police forces choose cars that are both fast and safe. Many police forces across the United States use Dodge Chargers. Chargers used by police have even better suspension and safety features than those made for regular customers.

Dodge Chargers are already heavy. Sirens, lights, radios, electronics, and police equipment make them even heavier. The ability to quickly and safely stop a heavy car traveling at high speeds is just as important as moving fast. The heavy-duty brakes used in police Chargers allow the car to stop much more quickly than normal vehicles.

GET THE FACTS!

The Dodge Charger can easily reach speeds of 150 miles (240 km) per hour, making it one of the fastest police cars on the road. In speed tests, a police Charger with a Hemi easily beat police cars from several other companies!

POLICE CHARGERS HAVE PUSH BUMPERS, OR PUSH BARS, ADDED TO THE FRONT. THESE CAN BE USED TO PUSH ANOTHER VEHICLE OUT OF THE ROAD OR EVEN KNOCK OVER FENCES OR GATES DURING A POLICE CHASE.

A CLASSIC FOR Collectors

For a long time, classic car collectors were interested only in rare second-generation Dodge Chargers. In 2015, a 1969 Dodge Charger Daytona—one of only 501 built—sold for $900,000! In recent years, the fastback Charger of the first generation has gained attention too.

GET THE FACTS!

The 2020 Dodge Charger SRT Hellcat Widebody Daytona 50th Anniversary Edition was built to honor the 1969 Charger Daytonas. This amazing car boasts 717 horsepower—much more muscle than the original Daytonas! Dodge plans to build only 501 of these powerhouse vehicles.

CLASSIC CAR SHOWS ARE A GREAT WAY TO ADMIRE CARS UP CLOSE—AND ALSO LEARN A LOT ABOUT HOW A CAR WORKS.

People take great pride in restoring and displaying their classic Chargers at car shows and other events across the country. And for those looking for the comforts of today's cars, there are many models of modern Chargers to choose from. The Chargers of today are the classics of tomorrow!

Glossary

aerodynamic Having a shape that improves airflow around a car to increase its speed.

classic Describing something that is considered one of the best of its kind or something that has become popular over time.

cruise control A technology in a car that a driver can use to make the vehicle continue at a chosen speed.

design The plan or form of something.

emblem A sign that represents an object, idea, group, or quality.

fender Any of the corner parts of the body of a car, especially those that surround the wheels.

front-wheel drive A system that gives engine power to the front wheels of a car.

fuel-efficient The quality of being able to operate using little fuel, or without waste.

hatchback A car design in which the trunk lid is replaced with a door that opens upward and usually includes the rear window.

horsepower A unit used to measure the power of an engine.

sedan A car with front and back seats, two or four doors, an enclosed body, and a permanent top.

suspension A system of springs and other parts on a car that reduces the shaking and bumping caused by uneven surfaces.

technology A machine, piece of equipment, or process that is created by the latest scientific tools and methods.

FOR MORE INFORMATION

BOOKS

Grout, Frank. *Dodge Charger*. North Mankato, MN: Rourke Educational Media, 2016.

Harrington, Denis J. *Dream Cars: Can You Picture Yourself in One?* Broomall, PA: Mason Crest, 2018.

Oachs, Emily Rose. *Dodge Charger R/T*. Minneapolis, MN: Bellwether Media, 2017.

WEBSITES

Dodge Charger
www.dodge.com/charger.html
Check out the latest about the newest Chargers.

10 Most Sought-After Classic Muscle Cars
musclecars.howstuffworks.com/classic-muscle-cars/10-most-wanted-classic-muscle-cars.htm
The Charger is on this cool classic cars list!

Publisher's note to educators and parents: Our editors have carefully reviewed these websites to ensure that they are suitable for students. Many websites change frequently, however, and we cannot guarantee that a site's future contents will continue to meet our high standards of quality and educational value. Be advised that students should be closely supervised whenever they access the internet.

Index